CELPIP LISTENING STRATEGIES

Tips & Strategies with Practice Questions & Answers

Ali Rastegari

1

CELPIP Listening Overview

In the CELPIP test, the listening section is divided into **6 tasks**, each designed to assess different aspects of your listening skills. You have **47-55 minutes** to complete the Listening Test. Let's take an in-depth look at each task, including the format, time allocation, and what you can expect.

Part 1: Listening to Problem Solving (8 Questions)
In this task, you will listen to a conversation between two people discussing a problem or a situation that needs a solution. You will be provided with multiple-choice questions related to the conversation. Your task is to select the best answer based on the information provided. This task evaluates your ability to understand conversations and draw conclusions.

Part 2: Listening to Daily Life Conversation (5 Questions)
Task 2 focuses on real-life situations you might encounter in your daily routine. You will listen to several short conversations or monologues and answer multiple-choice questions. The questions assess your comprehension of spoken English, including understanding details, main ideas, and implied meanings.

Part 3: Listening for Information (6 Questions)
In this task, you will listen to various speakers providing information, such as announcements, news reports, or instructions. You will answer multiple-choice questions based on the content of the audio. Task 3 evaluates your ability to gather specific details, make inferences, and identify key information accurately.

Part 4: Listening to a News Item (5 Questions)
Task 4 presents a news report on a current or topical issue. You will listen to the report and answer multiple-choice questions that assess your understanding of the main ideas, details, and the speaker's perspective. This task evaluates your ability to

comprehend and analyze spoken news items.

Part 5: Listening to a Discussion (8 Questions)

In Task 5, you will listen to a conversation among multiple speakers discussing a general topic or a problem. You will answer multiple-choice questions based on the dialogue, focusing on understanding the main ideas, speaker attitudes, and details. This task assesses your ability to comprehend extended conversations and follow multiple speakers.

Part 6: Listening to Viewpoints (6 Questions)

The final task, Part 6, presents a monologue expressing different viewpoints on a specific topic. You will answer multiple-choice questions that evaluate your understanding of the speaker's opinions, arguments, and supporting details. This task assesses your ability to comprehend and analyze spoken opinions and arguments.

It is important to note that the time allocations provided for each task are approximate and can vary slightly. Each task includes an introductory statement, audio playback, and question answering time.

Overall, the listening section of the CELPIP test assesses your ability to understand various spoken English contexts, ranging from everyday conversations to news items and discussions. By familiarizing yourself with the format of each task and practicing actively, you can enhance your listening skills and perform well on the CELPIP test.

Part 1: Listening to Problem-Solving (8 Questions)

Part 1 of the CELPIP Listening test, known as "Listening to Problem-Solving," assesses your ability to comprehend and analyze conversations involving problem-solving situations.

Here's a detailed breakdown of this section, including the time allocation, number of questions, and strategies to achieve a high score:

In this task, you will listen to a conversation between two individuals who are not acquainted with each other.

One person will present a problem, and the other, who represents an organization or public service, will provide assistance and help resolve the issue. The conversation is divided into three sections.

Time Allocation:

You will be given approximately 8 minutes to listen to the entire conversation and answer the corresponding questions. The audio will be played only once, so it's crucial to stay focused and attentive throughout.

Number of Questions:

Part 1 consists of a total of **8 questions**. After each section of the conversation, you will answer two or three multiple-choice questions. The questions may include response options in the form of words or pictures.

8 Tips and Strategies for Achieving a High Score

1. Familiarize Yourself with the Format: Prior to the test, become acquainted with the structure and question types of Part 1. Understanding what to expect will help you navigate the conversation more effectively.

2. Develop Active Listening Skills: Train yourself to listen actively by focusing on the main ideas, opinions expressed, and key details. Pay attention to the tone, emotions, and intentions of the speakers, as these elements can provide valuable context.

3. Take Notes: While listening to the conversation, jot down important keywords, phrases, or key details that may assist you in answering the questions accurately. Effective note-taking can improve your retention and aid in answering questions more efficiently.

4. Analyze the Problem and Solution: Understand the problem presented and the proposed solution. Analyze the conversation to identify the main points and the steps involved in resolving the issue. This will help you grasp the overall context and make informed choices when answering the questions.

5. Identify Speaker Attitudes and Opinions: Pay attention to the attitudes, opinions, and perspectives expressed by the speakers. This will allow you to choose the most appropriate response that aligns with the conversation.

6. Practice Active Listening: Engage in regular practice sessions that involve listening to conversations, analyzing them, and answering related questions. Focus on improving your comprehension, inference-making, and decision-making skills within the given time limit.

7. Time Management: Allocate sufficient time for each question, ensuring that you have ample opportunity to read and understand the options before making your selection. Avoid spending too much time on a single question to maintain a steady pace throughout the section.

8. Review and Revise: If time permits, review your answers before moving on to the next question. Verify if your responses align with the information provided in the conversation.

By employing these strategies and practicing actively, you can enhance your performance in Part 1 of the Listening section and work towards achieving a high score on the CELPIP test.

Remember to stay focused, manage your time effectively, and engage in regular practice to familiarize yourself with the format and optimize your listening skills.

Practice 1

You will hear a conversation between a man and a woman. The man is a librarian, and the woman is a library visitor trying to find a specific book.

Librarian: Good afternoon! How can I assist you today?
Visitor: Hi there! I'm looking for a book called "The Art of Photography." Do you have it in your collection?
Librarian: Let me check for you. Could you please provide me with the author's name?
Visitor: Yes, the author is John Thompson.
Librarian: Ah, yes! We do have that book. It's in the non-fiction section on the third floor. Just take the elevator and turn right when you get to the third floor. You'll find it on the second shelf from the left.
Visitor: Perfect! Thank you so much for your help.

Q1) What is the woman trying to find?
A) Fiction books
B) Children's books
C) Non-fiction book on photography
D) Poetry collection

Q2) What best describes the librarian's response?
A) He isn't sure.
B) He asks for the book's title.
C) He provides the book's location.
D) He suggests checking another library.

Q3) Where will the woman find the book?
A) Fiction section on the second floor
B) Children's section on the first floor
C) Non-fiction section on the third floor
D) Poetry section on the fourth floor

Visitor: Excuse me, I went to the third floor, but I couldn't find the book "The Art of Photography." Can you please help me again?

Librarian: I apologize for the confusion. Let me check our database again. Oh, it seems there was an error in the system. The book is actually in the photography section on the second floor, not the third floor. I'm sorry for the inconvenience.
Visitor: No problem. Thank you for clarifying.

Q4) What was the problem the visitor encountered?
A) The book was missing from the library.
B) The book was in the wrong section.
C) The book was checked out by someone else.
D) The book had a damaged cover.

Q5) How did the librarian resolve the issue?
A) He apologized for the inconvenience.
B) He offered to order the book from another library.
C) He provided the correct location of the book.
D) He suggested looking for a different book.

Q6) Where is the book "The Art of Photography" located?
A) Fiction section on the second floor
B) Children's section on the first floor
C) Non-fiction section on the third floor
D) Photography section on the second floor

Librarian: I found the book for you. It's on the second floor, in the photography section, on the third shelf from the right. You'll easily spot it; it has a blue cover.
Visitor: Thank you so much! I'll head there right away.

Q7) How did the librarian describe the book's location?
A) Fiction section, third shelf from the right
B) Children's section, second shelf from the left
C) Non-fiction section, fourth shelf from the right
D) Photography section, third shelf from the right

Q8) Will the visitor find the book?
A) No, it's missing from the library.
B) No, it's located in a different library branch.

C) Yes, and it's on the second floor.
D) Yes, but it's on the fourth shelf from the right.

Answer key:

Q1) C
Q2) C
Q3) C
Q4) B
Q5) C
Q6) D
Q7) D
Q8) C

Practice 2

You will hear a conversation between a man and a woman. The woman is a traveller looking for a specific location in a city, and the man is a local resident offering directions.

Man: Excuse me, can I help you find something?
Woman: Yes, please. I'm trying to find the nearest post office. Do you know where it is?
Man: Sure, there's a post office just a few blocks away from here. It's on Main Street, right next to the bank.
Woman: Is it the one with the blue sign?
Man: No, the one with the blue sign is the library. The post office has a red sign, and it's a bit further down the street.
Woman: Oh, I think I passed by it earlier. Is there a park nearby?
Man: Yes, there's a small park just across the street from the post office. You can't miss it.
Woman: Great! Thank you so much for your help.

Q1) What is the woman looking for?
A) Bank
B) Library
C) Park
D) Post office

Q2) How does the man know the directions?
A) He lives near the post office.
B) He saw the woman earlier.
C) He works at the library.
D) He is a local resident.

Q3) Where is the post office located?
A) Next to the library.
B) Across the street from the park.
C) On Main Street, near the bank.
D) A few blocks away from the man's house.

Woman: Excuse me again. I followed your directions, but I can't seem to find the post office.

Man: Oh, I apologize for the confusion. I made a mistake. The post office is actually on Elm Street, not Main Street.

Woman: Elm Street? That's not what you said before.

Man: I'm really sorry for the inconvenience. Let me correct the directions for you. Go back to the intersection and take a right turn onto Elm Street. The post office will be on your left, just after the grocery store.

Woman: Okay, I'll give it another try. Thanks for your help.

Q4) What did the man apologize for?
A) Giving wrong directions.
B) Forgetting the street name.
C) Misplacing the post office.
D) Causing inconvenience.

Q5) Where is the post office actually located?
A) On Main Street, near the bank.
B) Next to the library.
C) Across the street from the park.
D) On Elm Street, after the grocery store.

Q6) What should the woman do to find the post office?
A) Take a left turn onto Elm Street.
B) Return to the intersection and go straight.
C) Continue on Main Street and look for the blue sign.
D) Ask another person for directions.

Man: Excuse me, did you find the post office?

Woman: Yes, I finally found it. Thank you for correcting the directions.

Man: You're welcome. Is there anything else I can help you with?

Woman: Actually, I'm also looking for a good restaurant nearby. Do you have any recommendations?

Man: There's a popular Italian restaurant just a block away from the post office. It's called "La Trattoria." You should try their pasta dishes.

Woman: That sounds perfect. I'll check it out. Thanks again for your assistance.
Man: No problem at all. Enjoy your meal!

Q7) What is the woman looking for now?
A) Library
B) Post office
C) Restaurant
D) Grocery store

Q8) Where is the recommended restaurant located?
A) Near the park.
B) Across the street from the post office.
C) Next to the bank.
D) Just a block away from the post office.

Answer key:

Q1) C
Q2) D
Q3) A
Q4) A
Q5) D
Q6) D
Q7) C
Q8) D

Practice 3

You will hear a conversation between a woman and a man. The woman is a customer at a store, and the man is an employee helping her find a lost item.

Man: Can I help you with something?
Woman: Yes, I lost my necklace somewhere in the store. I've been searching everywhere, but I can't find it.
Man: I'll do my best to assist you. Can you describe the necklace? Maybe I can remember seeing it.
Woman: It's a silver pendant necklace with a blue gemstone in the shape of a heart.
Man: I think I might have seen it at the jewelry counter. Let me check for you.
Woman: Oh, thank you so much!

Q1) What is the woman trying to find?
A) Earrings
B) Bracelet
C) Necklace
D) Ring

Q2) What will the man do to help the woman?
A) Look in his bag.
B) Call the security guard.
C) Check the jewelry counter.
D) Ask other customers.

Q3) How would the woman describe her necklace?
A) Silver pendant with a blue heart-shaped gemstone.
B) Gold chain with a red heart-shaped gemstone.
C) Platinum pendant with a green circular gemstone.
D) Copper chain with a yellow square gemstone.

Man: I found your necklace! It was indeed at the jewelry counter. Here you go.
Woman: Oh, thank goodness! I was so worried. I appreciate your

help.

Man: No problem. I'm glad we found it. Is there anything else I can assist you with?

Woman: No, that's all. Thank you again for your assistance.

Q4) Where was the necklace found?
A) In the woman's bag.
B) At the jewelry counter.
C) Near the store entrance.
D) Inside a clothing rack.

Q5) How does the woman feel after finding her necklace?
A) Relieved
B) Frustrated
C) Annoyed
D) Indifferent

Q6) Does the woman need any further assistance?
A) Yes, she has another item to find.
B) No, she is satisfied with the help.
C) Yes, she wants to report the lost item.
D) No, she wants to leave the store immediately.

Man: You're welcome. Have a great day!
Woman: You too. Thanks again!

Q7) How does the man respond to the woman's gratitude?
A) "You're welcome. Have a great day!"
B) "No problem. It's my job."
C) "I'm glad I could help. Take care."
D) "You're welcome. Come back anytime."

Q8) Is the conversation between the man and the woman finished?
A) Yes, they both express gratitude and end the conversation.
B) No, the woman wants to discuss another issue.
C) Yes, the woman wants to leave the store immediately.
D) No, the man wants to offer additional assistance.

Answer key:

Q1) C
Q2) C
Q3) A
Q4) B
Q5) A
Q6) B
Q7) A
Q8) A

Part 2: Listening to Daily Life Conversation (5 Questions)

In the CELPIP test, Part 2 of the Listening section focuses on "Listening to Daily Life Conversation." This part assesses your ability to understand informal conversations that you might encounter in everyday situations. It measures your comprehension of spoken English in various contexts such as social gatherings, workplace interactions, and personal conversations.

Number of Questions:

You're going to have 5 minutes to listen to the conversation and answer the **5 questions**. The questions assess a range of listening skills, including understanding the main idea, specific details, relationships between speakers, and inferred meaning.

8 Tips and Strategies for Achieving a High Score

1. Familiarize yourself with different conversational styles: Practice listening to a variety of informal conversations, including casual conversations between friends, workplace discussions, and social interactions. This exposure will help you become comfortable with different accents, speaking speeds, and vocabulary used in everyday conversations.

2. Improve your note-taking skills: While listening, take brief notes to help you remember important details. Focus on keywords, main ideas, and any specific information provided. Effective note-taking can aid in answering the questions accurately.

3. Pay attention to the context: Understand the context of the conversation, including the speakers' relationship, location, and purpose of the discussion. This background knowledge will assist you in better understanding the dialogue and answering related questions correctly.

4. Predict and anticipate information: Before listening to the conversation, quickly skim through the questions to get an idea of what information you need to listen for. This strategy will help you stay focused and actively listen for the relevant details.

5. Utilize the pause effectively: During the brief pause between conversations, quickly read the questions and underline or highlight keywords. This will enable you to focus on finding the specific information while listening to the conversation.

6. Develop your listening skills: Regularly practice listening to a wide range of English audio materials, such as podcasts, interviews, TV shows, and movies. This will improve your overall listening comprehension and enhance your ability to understand conversational English.

7. Manage your time effectively: Allocate your time wisely during the test. Remember to pace yourself, as each conversation and set of questions should be completed within the given timeframe. Avoid spending too much time on any single question.

8. Review and check your answers: Once you have completed all the questions for each conversation, take a moment to review your answers before moving on to the next conversation. Check for any errors or possible corrections.

By following these tips and strategies, you can enhance your performance in Part 2 of the Listening section of the CELPIP test and achieve a high score. Regular practice, active listening, and familiarity with different conversational contexts will contribute to your success on this section of the exam.

Practice 1

You will hear a conversation between two friends discussing their plans for the upcoming weekend.

John: Hey, what are your plans for the weekend?

Sina: I'm not sure yet. I've been feeling a bit burnt out lately, so I think I might take it easy and relax at home.

John: That sounds like a good idea. Sometimes we all need a break to recharge. Are you planning on doing anything specific?

Sina: Well, I've been wanting to catch up on some reading. I have a few books that I've been meaning to dive into. It would be nice to curl up on the couch with a good book and just escape into different worlds for a while.

John: That sounds perfect for some relaxation time. Any particular genre or book you're looking forward to reading?

Sina: I enjoy various genres, but I think I'll start with a mystery novel this time. I love getting engrossed in a suspenseful plot and trying to solve the mystery along with the characters. It's like a mental workout and entertainment combined.

John: That's a great choice! It can be so exciting to follow the twists and turns of a good mystery. Do you have any specific books in mind?

Sina: Yes, I recently heard about a new release that's been receiving rave reviews. It's called "The Silent Detective" by a popular author. The synopsis sounded intriguing, and the reviews mention that it's a real page-turner. I'm really looking forward to diving into it.

John: Oh, I've heard about that book too! It's been getting a lot of buzz lately. It seems like the perfect choice for a weekend of reading. I might even pick up a copy myself and we can discuss it later.

Sina: That would be fantastic! I always enjoy discussing books with you. It adds another layer of enjoyment to the reading experience when you can share your thoughts and theories with someone else.

John: Absolutely! It's like having our own mini-book club. So, besides reading, do you have any other plans for the weekend?

Sina: Not really, just some self-care activities like taking long walks, maybe indulging in a bubble bath, and catching up on some much-needed sleep. It's all about recharging and finding balance.

John: That sounds like the perfect weekend plan. I hope you have a relaxing and enjoyable time. Remember to take care of yourself and prioritize your well-being.

Sina: Thank you! I definitely will. And what about you? What are your plans for the weekend?

John: I'm actually thinking of going hiking. There's a beautiful trail nearby that I've been wanting to explore. Nature always helps me unwind and clear my mind.

Sina: That sounds wonderful! Enjoy the fresh air and the beauty of nature. It's a great way to recharge as well. Maybe we can catch up afterward and share our weekend experiences.

John: Definitely! Let's plan on that. It will be great to reconnect and hear about each other's weekend adventures.

Q1) What does Sina plan to do on the weekend?
A) Catch up on reading
B) Go hiking
C) Visit friends
D) Do some self-care activities

Q2) What genre does Sina prefer for reading?
A) Mystery
B) Romance

C) Science fiction
D) Biography

Q3) What book does Sina mention?
A) "The History of Time"
B) "The Enchanting Garden"
C) "The Lost World"
D) "The Silent Detective"

Q4) How does John plan to unwind on the weekend?
A) By watching movies
B) By catching up on sleep
C) By visiting a spa
D) By going hiking

Q5) What do John and Sina plan to do after their weekend activities?
A) Attend a concert
B) Go shopping together
C) Meet up and share their experiences
D) Have a picnic in the park

Answer key:

Q1) A) Catch up on reading
Q2) A) Mystery
Q3) D) "The Silent Detective"
Q4) D) By going hiking
Q5) C) Meet up and share their experiences

Practice 2

You will hear a conversation between two colleagues discussing their plans for an upcoming business trip.

Emily: Hi Mark, have you made any arrangements for our business trip next week?

Mark: Not yet, Emily. I've been swamped with work, but I'll get on it soon. Do you have any suggestions for accommodations?

Emily: Actually, I found a great hotel near the conference venue. It has excellent reviews and offers convenient amenities for business travellers like us.

Mark: That's fantastic! A comfortable and convenient hotel would make our trip much smoother. Could you please share the details with me?

Emily: Sure, it's called "The Business Haven." It's a modern hotel with spacious rooms and a dedicated workspace. They also have a well-equipped business center, which would be perfect for any last-minute preparations.

Mark: Sounds ideal for our needs. I appreciate you taking the initiative to find a suitable place. How about transportation to the conference?

Emily: I was thinking of renting a car for the duration of our stay. It would give us flexibility and make it easier to get around the city, especially considering the busy schedule we have.

Mark: Renting a car sounds like a smart choice. It'll save us time and ensure we're punctual for all our meetings. Do you have any recommendations for a reliable car rental agency?

Emily: Yes, I've looked into a few options, and "DriveSmart Rentals" seems to have a good reputation. They offer competitive rates and a wide selection of vehicles. I'll share their contact information with you so we can make the reservation together.

Mark: Perfect, I'll make a note of it. Thanks for doing the research, Emily. Now, regarding meals during the trip, any preferences or dietary restrictions I should be aware of?

Emily: Not particularly. I'm open to trying local cuisine and exploring new restaurants. However, I'll let you know if I have any specific dietary requirements closer to the trip.

Mark: Sounds good. It would be great to experience the local food scene and perhaps even network with clients over dinner. Let's keep our options open and take recommendations from locals if possible.

Emily: Absolutely, networking opportunities shouldn't be missed. We should also plan some downtime during the trip. Any thoughts on what we can do to relax after a busy day?

Mark: I agree, downtime is crucial. Since we'll be in a new city, it would be nice to explore some attractions or visit a nearby park to unwind. We could also check if there are any cultural events happening during our stay.

Emily: That sounds like a plan. Taking in the local culture and sights would add a refreshing touch to our trip. I'll do some research on notable attractions and events in the area.

Mark: Excellent, I'm looking forward to it. Lastly, let's make sure we have all the necessary documents and materials prepared before we leave. We don't want any last-minute surprises.

Emily: Absolutely, I'll double-check our travel itineraries, conference schedules, and any presentation materials we need. Organization and preparedness are key to a successful business trip.

Mark: Couldn't agree more. With our thorough planning and attention to detail, this business trip is bound to be a success.

Thank you for your contributions, Emily.

Emily: You're welcome, Mark. It's a team effort, and I'm glad we're on the same page. Let's make this trip productive and enjoyable.

Q1) What did Emily find for accommodations during the business trip?
A) A hotel near the conference venue.
B) A bed and breakfast in the countryside.
C) A luxury resort by the beach.
D) A budget-friendly hostel in the city.

Q2) What amenities does "The Business Haven" hotel offer?
A) A spa and wellness center.
B) A fitness facility.
C) A dedicated workspace and business center.
D) A rooftop restaurant and bar.

Q3) How do Emily and Mark plan to get around the city during the trip?
A) By renting a car.
B) By taking public transportation.
C) By walking.
D) By using ride-sharing services.

Q4) Which car rental agency did Emily recommend?
A) "Rent-a-Ride"
B) "DriveSmart Rentals"
C) "Easy Wheels"
D) "Swift Cars"

Q5) What do Emily and Mark plan to do during their downtime on the trip?
A) Relax at the hotel spa.
B) Explore local attractions.
C) Attend cultural events.
D) Participate in team-building activities.

Answer key:

Q1) A) A hotel near the conference venue.

Q2) C) A dedicated workspace and business center.

Q3) A) By renting a car.

Q4) B) "DriveSmart Rentals"

Q5) B) Explore local attractions.

Practice 3

You will hear a conversation between two friends discussing their plans for the upcoming weekend.

Sarah: Hey, what are your plans for the weekend?

Emma: I'm not sure yet. I've been feeling a bit exhausted lately, so I think I might take it easy and relax at home.

Sarah: That sounds like a good idea. Sometimes we all need a break to recharge. Are you planning on doing anything specific?

Emma: Well, I've been wanting to work on some art projects. I have a few canvases that I've been meaning to paint. It would be nice to unleash my creativity and spend some time with my brushes and paints.

Sarah: That sounds perfect for some relaxation time. Any particular style or theme you're looking forward to exploring?

Emma: I enjoy experimenting with different styles, but this time I think I'll start with abstract art. I love the freedom it offers and how it allows me to express my emotions and thoughts in a unique way. It's like a visual journey.

Sarah: That's a great choice! Abstract art can be so fascinating and open to interpretation. Do you have any specific ideas in mind?

Emma: Yes, I've been inspired by nature lately, so I'm planning to create a series of paintings that capture the beauty and tranquility of landscapes. I want to explore different color palettes and techniques to evoke different moods.

Sarah: Oh, I can't wait to see your creations! Nature-inspired abstract art sounds amazing. It's always so interesting to see how artists interpret the world around them. Maybe we can have a mini art exhibition with your paintings.

Emma: That would be fantastic! I'd love to showcase my artwork and hear people's interpretations. It adds another layer of depth to the creative process when you can engage with others.

Sarah: Absolutely! It's like opening a window to different perspectives. So, besides art, do you have any other plans for the weekend?

Emma: Not really, just some self-care activities like practicing yoga, maybe pampering myself with a facial mask, and spending quality time with my dog. It's all about taking care of my well-being and finding inner peace.

Sarah: That sounds like the perfect weekend plan. I hope you have a rejuvenating and fulfilling time. Remember to prioritize self-care and nourish your soul.

Emma: Thank you! I definitely will. And what about you? What are your plans for the weekend?

Sarah: I'm actually thinking of visiting a nearby farmers market. I love exploring local produce, trying out new flavors, and supporting local farmers. It's a great way to reconnect with nature and the community.

Emma: That sounds wonderful! Enjoy the fresh fruits and vegetables, and the vibrant atmosphere. It's a great way to recharge and appreciate the simple pleasures in life. Maybe we can meet up afterward and share our weekend experiences.

Sarah: Definitely! Let's plan on that. It will be great to catch up, see your artwork, and hear about each other's weekend adventures.

Q1) What does Emma plan to do on the weekend?
A) Catch up on reading
B) Work on art projects
C) Visit a farmers market
D) Practice yoga

Q2) What style of art does Emma prefer?

A) Realism
B) Abstract
C) Impressionism
D) Surrealism

Q3) What theme does Emma mention for her artwork?
A) Portraits of animals
B) Cityscapes
C) Landscapes inspired by nature
D) Still life

Q4) How does Sarah plan to unwind on the weekend?
A) By going to the beach
B) By visiting a spa
C) By trying out new recipes
D) By visiting a farmers market

Q5) What do Sarah and Emma plan to do after their weekend activities?
A) Attend a concert
B) Go shopping together
C) Meet up and share their experiences
D) Have a picnic in the park

Answer key:

Q1) A) Catch up on reading
Q2) B) Abstract
Q3) C) Landscapes inspired by nature
Q4) D) By visiting a farmers market
Q5) C) Meet up and share their experiences

Part 3: Listening for Information (6 Questions)

Part 3 of the CELPIP listening test, "Listening for Information," focuses on your ability to comprehend and extract specific information from a longer conversation or presentation. This section assesses your listening skills in real-life situations where you need to gather details and facts.

In the Listening for Information section, you will typically hear a longer conversation or presentation, such as an interview, lecture, or radio program. The recording will be played only once, and you will need to listen carefully to gather the necessary information to answer the questions.

The length of the audio recording can vary, but it is typically around 2-3 minutes long. Within this timeframe, you will need to listen attentively and grasp the details provided.

After listening to the recording, you will be given a set of multiple-choice questions related to the content you just heard. You will have to select the correct option based on the information provided in the audio. The questions can cover various aspects, such as specific details, main ideas, opinions, comparisons, or inferences.

Timing and Number of Questions:

In this listening part you will listen to a long conversation between 2 people. You're going to have about 6 minutes to listen to the conversation and answer **6 questions**.

It is crucial to manage your time effectively to ensure you have enough time to carefully read the questions, analyze the answer choices, and select the most appropriate option based on the information you heard.

8 Tips and Strategies for Achieving a High Score

1. Familiarize yourself with the question types: Become familiar with the different types of questions you may encounter in Part 3, such as matching information, completing a form, or selecting the best response. Understanding the question formats will help you respond more efficiently.

2. Skim the questions before listening: Quickly skim through the questions before the recording starts. This will give you an idea of the type of information you need to listen for and help you stay focused during the recording.

3. Take notes: While listening to the recording, make brief notes or keywords related to the information being provided. This will assist you in recalling the details when answering the questions.

4. Listen for specific details: Pay close attention to the specific details, such as *names, dates, numbers, locations, or any key information* mentioned in the recording. Try to extract the relevant information and eliminate distractions to accurately answer the questions.

5. Read the options carefully: Read all the options before selecting your answer. Sometimes, similar-sounding choices may be provided, and careful reading will help you identify the correct response.

6. Use the process of elimination: If you are unsure about the correct answer, use the process of elimination. Eliminate options that are clearly incorrect, and focus on the remaining choices to improve your chances of selecting the right answer.

7. Practice active listening: Practice active listening skills in your daily life. Engage in conversations, listen to news broadcasts, watch movies or TV shows, and try to comprehend the main ideas and key details. This will enhance your overall listening abilities.

8. Practice with sample tests: Familiarize yourself with the format and question types by practicing with sample tests or past papers. This will help you become more comfortable with the structure of Part 3 and improve your time management skills.

Remember to stay focused, maintain a calm demeanour, and pace yourself throughout the Listening section. By employing these tips and strategies, you can maximize your chances of achieving a high score in Part 3 of the CELPIP Listening test.

Practice 1

You will hear a conversation. A woman is interviewing a man about sustainable living and eco-friendly practices.

Woman: Hello, Mr. Anderson. Thank you for joining us today to discuss sustainable living and eco-friendly practices. To start off, why do you think it's important for individuals to adopt a sustainable lifestyle?

Man: Thank you for having me. Adopting a sustainable lifestyle is crucial for preserving our planet for future generations. It's about minimizing our impact on the environment by making conscious choices that promote conservation and reduce waste.

Woman: That's a great perspective. Can you provide some examples of sustainable practices that individuals can incorporate into their daily lives?

Man: Absolutely. There are several simple steps that can make a big difference. For instance, reducing water consumption by taking shorter showers or installing low-flow faucets. Using energy-efficient appliances and opting for renewable energy sources like solar power is another effective way to contribute.

Woman: Those are excellent suggestions. What about waste reduction?

Man: Waste reduction is key. People can start by recycling and composting to divert waste from landfills. Avoiding single-use plastics and opting for reusable alternatives, such as shopping bags, water bottles, and coffee cups, also plays a significant role in reducing waste.

Woman: I completely agree. Now, let's talk about transportation. How can individuals make their travel more eco-friendly?

Man: Choosing alternative transportation methods like biking, walking, or using public transportation whenever possible is a great way to reduce carbon emissions. For longer distances, carpooling or using electric vehicles are greener options.

Woman: Excellent suggestions. Now, let's shift our focus to sustainable food choices. What can individuals do in that regard?

Man: Sustainable food choices are essential. Opting for locally sourced, organic produce reduces the carbon footprint associated with long-distance transportation and chemical-intensive farming. Supporting farmers' markets and growing your own food, even in small spaces, can make a positive impact.

Woman: Those are wonderful ideas. Finally, do you have any advice for individuals who want to embrace a more sustainable lifestyle?

Man: I would advise starting small and gradually incorporating sustainable practices into daily routines. Educate yourself about the environmental impact of your choices and seek out sustainable alternatives. It's also helpful to connect with like-minded individuals and organizations to learn and share experiences.

Woman: Thank you for sharing such valuable insights, Mr. Anderson. Your expertise in sustainable living is truly inspiring.

Q1) What is the topic of the conversation?
A) Sustainable living and eco-friendly practices.
B) The benefits of gardening.
C) The importance of exercise.
D) Home decoration tips.

Q2) Why is adopting a sustainable lifestyle important?
A) To reduce water consumption.
B) To minimize the impact on the environment.
C) To improve personal well-being.
D) To save money on energy bills.

Q3) What is one example of a sustainable practice mentioned?

A) Installing low-flow faucets.
B) Using disposable water bottles.
C) Taking long showers.
D) Using non-renewable energy sources.

Q4) How can individuals make their travel more eco-friendly?
A) By driving alone in a gas-guzzling car.
B) By using alternative transportation methods.
C) By avoiding public transportation.
D) By taking long-distance flights.

Q5) What is one suggestion for making sustainable food choices?
A) Supporting local farmers' markets.
B) Buying imported produce.
C) Choosing heavily processed foods.
D) Growing food on large-scale farms.

Q6) What advice does the man give to individuals interested in a sustainable lifestyle?
A) Start small and gradually incorporate sustainable practices.
B) Ignore the impact of personal choices on the environment.
C) Rely on others to make eco-friendly decisions.
D) Avoid connecting with like-minded individuals.

Answer key:

Q1) A
Q2) B
Q3) A
Q4) B
Q5) A
Q6) A

Practice 2

You will hear a conversation. A woman is speaking with a man about the benefits of learning a second language.

Woman: Hi, John. I heard you've been learning a second language. What made you decide to take up this endeavor?

Man: Hey, Sarah. Yes, I recently started learning Spanish. There are so many reasons why I wanted to learn a second language. Firstly, it opens up a whole new world of communication and connections with people from different cultures.

Woman: That's true. Learning a second language can certainly enhance your cultural understanding. Are there any other benefits you've experienced?

Man: Absolutely. It has improved my cognitive abilities and problem-solving skills. Learning a new language requires you to think flexibly and adapt to different linguistic structures, which can enhance overall mental agility.

Woman: That's fascinating. I've also heard that learning a second language can have positive effects on memory. Have you noticed any improvements in that area?

Man: Yes, definitely. Memorizing new vocabulary and grammar rules exercises my memory muscles. It's like a workout for the brain. Over time, I've noticed improvements in my memory retention and recall, not just for language-related information but also in everyday life.

Woman: That's impressive. I can see how learning a second language can have cognitive benefits. How about personal growth? Have you experienced any personal development through language learning?

Man: Absolutely. Learning a second language has pushed me out of my comfort zone and challenged me to embrace new experiences. It has boosted my confidence as I navigate conversations in a foreign language. It also helps me become more empathetic and understanding of different perspectives.

Woman: That's wonderful to hear. I can see how learning a second language can have a transformative impact on an individual. Are there any practical advantages to knowing a second language?

Man: Definitely. Knowing a second language can open up various professional opportunities. Many companies value employees who can communicate with clients and partners from different parts of the world. It also enhances cross-cultural communication skills, which are highly valuable in today's globalized world.

Woman: That's a great point. Language skills can certainly give you a competitive edge in the job market. Overall, it sounds like learning a second language has been a rewarding experience for you.

Man: Absolutely. I would encourage anyone to embark on the journey of learning a second language. It not only expands your horizons but also brings numerous personal and professional benefits.

Q1) What is the topic of the conversation?
A) The benefits of learning a second language.
B) The importance of cultural understanding.
C) The challenges of language learning.
D) The impact of bilingualism on memory.

Q2) What is one benefit the man mentions about learning a second language?
A) Improved physical fitness.
B) Enhanced problem-solving skills.
C) Increased musical abilities.
D) Expanded social media presence.

Q3) According to the conversation, how does learning a second language impact memory?

A) It has no effect on memory.
B) It improves memory retention and recall.
C) It reduces memory capabilities.
D) It enhances short-term memory only.

Q4) How does the man describe the personal growth aspect of language learning?
A) It boosts confidence and empathy.
B) It limits personal experiences.
C) It decreases social interactions.
D) It isolates individuals from others.

Q5) What practical advantages does the man mention for knowing a second language?
A) Better physical health.
B) More social media followers.
C) Enhanced cross-cultural communication skills.
D) Improved musical performances.

Q6) What is the man's overall opinion about learning a second language?
A) He strongly encourages it due to the various benefits.
B) He thinks it's unnecessary and time-consuming.
C) He believes it has no practical advantages.
D) He finds it challenging and not worth the effort.

Answer key:

Q1) A
Q2) B
Q3) B
Q4) A
Q5) C
Q6) A

Practice 3

You will hear a conversation between two friends discussing the benefits of regular exercise.

Friend 1: Hey, Sarah. I've noticed you've been hitting the gym quite regularly lately. What motivated you to start exercising?

Friend 2: Hi, Lisa. Yes, I've made it a priority to incorporate exercise into my routine. There are so many benefits that come with regular physical activity. Firstly, it improves overall health and fitness.

Friend 1: That's true. Regular exercise has numerous health benefits. Can you tell me more about it?

Friend 2: Absolutely. Exercise helps maintain a healthy weight, reduces the risk of chronic diseases such as heart disease and diabetes, and strengthens the immune system. It also promotes better sleep and boosts energy levels.

Friend 1: Those are some great advantages. I've also heard that exercise has positive effects on mental well-being. Have you experienced any mental benefits?

Friend 2: Definitely. Exercise releases endorphins, which are natural mood-boosting chemicals in the brain. It helps reduce stress, anxiety, and symptoms of depression. Personally, I've noticed a significant improvement in my mood and overall mental clarity since I started exercising regularly.

Friend 1: That's amazing. It seems like exercise has a positive impact on both physical and mental health. Are there any other benefits you've noticed?

Friend 2: Absolutely. Regular exercise helps improve strength and flexibility, enhances bone density, and reduces the risk of falls and injuries, especially as we age. It also provides an opportunity for social interaction if you engage in group exercises or team sports.

Friend 1: Ah, that's true. Exercise can be a great way to connect with others and build a sense of community. I can see why it's so important to incorporate physical activity into our lives.

Friend 2: Definitely. It's not just about the physical benefits but also about overall well-being. Plus, it can be a lot of fun and enjoyable. Finding an activity you love makes it easier to stay motivated and consistent.

Friend 1: That's a great point. So, what types of exercises have you been doing lately?

Friend 2: I've been mixing it up with a combination of cardio exercises like running and cycling, strength training with weights, and some yoga for flexibility and relaxation.

Friend 1: Sounds like a well-rounded routine. I might join you and start incorporating exercise into my own life. It's inspiring to hear about all these benefits.

Friend 2: That would be great, Lisa! We can even work out together and keep each other motivated. Remember, consistency is key when it comes to exercise.

Friend 1: Absolutely. Thank you for sharing all this valuable information, Sarah. I'm excited to start my fitness journey.

Q1) What is the topic of the conversation?
A) The benefits of regular exercise.
B) The importance of healthy eating.
C) The risks of a sedentary lifestyle.
D) The psychology of motivation.

Q2) What is one health benefit mentioned in the conversation?
A) Increased risk of chronic diseases.
B) Weakened immune system.
C) Sleep disorders.
D) Reduced risk of heart disease.

Q3) How does exercise impact mental well-being?
A) It increases stress and anxiety levels.
B) It worsens symptoms of depression.
C) It releases mood-boosting chemicals.
D) It decreases mental clarity.

Q4) Besides physical and mental benefits, what other advantages does exercise offer?
A) Enhanced sense of taste.
B) Improved memory retention.
C) Reduced bone density.
D) Opportunities for social interaction.

Q5) How does the conversation emphasize the importance of finding an exercise activity you enjoy?
A) It highlights the need for competition.
B) It promotes solo exercise routines.
C) It suggests group activities for social interaction.
D) It discourages consistency in workouts.

Q6) What types of exercises has Sarah been doing lately?
A) Cardio, strength training, and yoga.
B) Dancing, swimming, and hiking.
C) Pilates, meditation, and kickboxing.
D) Stretching, tai chi, and weightlifting.

Answer key:

Q1) A
Q2) D
Q3) C
Q4) D
Q5) C
Q6) A

Part 4: Listening to a News Item (5 Questions)

Part 4 of the CELPIP listening test is called "Listening to a News Item." In this section, you will listen to a news report or news-related conversation and answer questions based on the information provided. This part assesses your ability to understand and extract information from news sources.

In the Listening to a News Item section, you will typically hear a news report or a conversation between news presenters discussing a current event or news topic. The audio recording is usually around **1-2 minutes** long. The news item may include information about recent events, social issues, scientific discoveries, or any other relevant news topic.

You will be presented with five multiple-choice questions based on the content of the news item. These questions will test your understanding of the main ideas, specific details, opinions, and other relevant information from the news report. Each question will have four answer options, and you need to select the most appropriate one based on what you heard.

It is crucial to manage your time effectively to read the questions, listen to the audio carefully, and select the correct answer option within the given time limit.

To achieve a high score in the Listening to a News Item section, consider the following tips and strategies on the next page.

7 Tips and Strategies for Achieving a High Score

1. Familiarize yourself with different news topics: Stay updated with current events and news stories from various sources. This will help you become familiar with common news vocabulary and topics, making it easier to understand the content of the news item during the test.

2. Improve your listening skills: Practice listening to news reports or news-related conversations regularly. Focus on understanding the main ideas, supporting details, and the overall message conveyed in the news item. This will help you develop your listening comprehension skills and enhance your ability to extract information.

3. Take notes while listening: During the audio recording, take brief notes on key points, names, dates, or any important details. This will assist you in recalling the information and answering the questions accurately.

4. Pay attention to intonation and emphasis: Notice how the speakers emphasize certain words or phrases. This can provide clues to the importance or significance of the information being presented.

5. Read the questions carefully: Before listening to the news item, read the questions thoroughly. This will give you an idea of what information you need to listen for and help you focus your attention during the audio recording.

6. Eliminate incorrect answer choices: If you are unsure about the correct answer, try to eliminate any answer choices that are obviously incorrect. Narrowing down the options will increase your chances of selecting the correct answer.

7. Manage your time effectively: Keep track of the time available for answering the questions and allocate sufficient time for reading, listening, and selecting the answers. Practice time management during your preparation to ensure you can complete all the questions within the given time limit.

By following these tips and strategies, you can improve your performance in the Listening to a News Item section and achieve a higher score on the CELPIP listening test.

Practice 1

You will hear a news item about a breakthrough in renewable energy technology.

Speaker: In a major development for renewable energy, a team of scientists at GreenTech Innovations has announced a groundbreaking discovery. They have successfully developed a new type of solar panel that is significantly more efficient than traditional solar panels. This breakthrough has the potential to revolutionize the solar energy industry and address some of the limitations that have hindered its widespread adoption.

The new solar panel utilizes advanced nanotechnology and a unique design that allows it to capture and convert sunlight into electricity more efficiently than ever before. Initial tests have shown an impressive increase in energy conversion efficiency, which means that a smaller surface area of these new panels can generate the same amount of electricity as larger conventional panels.

Dr. Sarah Thompson, the lead scientist behind this innovation, explained that the key to the improved efficiency lies in the panel's ability to capture a broader spectrum of sunlight, including both visible and infrared wavelengths. This wider absorption range enhances the panel's performance even in low-light conditions, making it more versatile and reliable in various weather conditions.

GreenTech Innovations is currently working on scaling up the production of these advanced solar panels to meet the growing demand for renewable energy solutions. They anticipate that these panels will not only increase the viability of solar power for residential and commercial use but also have applications in other sectors such as electric vehicles and portable electronics.

This breakthrough holds significant promise for a greener and more sustainable future. It offers the potential to reduce reliance on fossil fuels and mitigate the environmental impact of energy generation. With further advancements and continued research, solar energy could become a more accessible and mainstream source of power globally.

Q1) The news item is about...
A) a breakthrough in renewable energy technology.
B) a new medical treatment.
C) advancements in nanotechnology.
D) the challenges of solar panel installation.

Q2) What makes the new solar panel more efficient?
A) Its smaller size.
B) Its ability to capture a broader spectrum of sunlight.
C) Its compatibility with electric vehicles.
D) Its lower production costs.

Q3) According to Dr. Sarah Thompson, what is the advantage of the new solar panel?
A) It is more affordable than conventional panels.
B) It can generate electricity in any weather condition.
C) It requires less maintenance.
D) It is easier to install.

Q4) What is GreenTech Innovations currently focused on?
A) Expanding their research team.
B) Exploring applications in portable electronics.
C) Reducing the production costs of solar panels.
D) Scaling up the production of the new solar panels.

Q5) What potential impact could the new solar panel have?
A) Decreasing the demand for fossil fuels.
B) Eliminating the need for other renewable energy sources.
C) Increasing global energy consumption.
D) Reducing the cost of electricity for consumers."

Answer key:

Q1) A

Q2) B
Q3) B
Q4) D
Q5) A

Practice 2

You will hear a news item about a new transportation technology called Hyperloop.

Speaker: In an exciting development in transportation, a company called TransLink has unveiled plans for a new high-speed transportation system known as Hyperloop. Hyperloop aims to revolutionize the way people travel by utilizing advanced magnetic levitation technology in a low-pressure tube, allowing for speeds of up to 700 miles per hour.

The system works by propelling specially designed pods through a vacuum-sealed tube, eliminating air resistance and enabling incredibly fast and efficient travel. This technology has the potential to dramatically reduce travel times and offer a more sustainable alternative to traditional modes of transportation.

TransLink's CEO, Sarah Johnson, spoke at a press conference, expressing her enthusiasm for the project. She highlighted the numerous benefits of Hyperloop, including its ability to connect distant cities and regions, ease traffic congestion, and reduce carbon emissions.

The initial plans involve constructing a Hyperloop route between two major cities, significantly reducing the travel time from hours to mere minutes. This project has garnered attention from both the public and private sectors, with several investors expressing interest in supporting its development.

While the Hyperloop technology is still in its early stages, TransLink is committed to conducting further research and feasibility studies to ensure its safety and viability. The company aims to collaborate with government agencies and experts to address regulatory and logistical challenges.

If successful, Hyperloop could transform the way people commute and travel long distances, making it more efficient, environmentally friendly, and convenient.

Q1) The news item is about...
A) a new high-speed transportation system called Hyperloop.
B) advancements in magnetic levitation technology.
C) the impact of air resistance on transportation.
D) reducing travel times in major cities.

Q2) How does Hyperloop achieve high speeds?
A) By utilizing magnetic levitation technology.
B) By reducing air resistance in the tube.
C) By using specially designed pods.
D) By constructing a vacuum-sealed tube.

Q3) According to the news item, what are some benefits of Hyperloop?
A) Connecting distant cities and regions, reducing traffic congestion, and decreasing carbon emissions.
B) Increasing air resistance and improving traditional modes of transportation.
C) Generating interest from private investors and government agencies.
D) Conducting feasibility studies and addressing regulatory challenges.

Q4) What stage is the Hyperloop technology currently in?
A) Early stages with ongoing research and feasibility studies.
B) Final stages of development and implementation.
C) Already operational between two major cities.
D) Facing regulatory and logistical challenges.

Q5) What potential impact could Hyperloop have on transportation?
A) Dramatically reducing travel times and offering a more sustainable alternative.
B) Eliminating the need for other modes of transportation.
C) Increasing traffic congestion in major cities.
D) Expanding public transportation networks."

Answer key:

Q1) A
Q2) A
Q3) A
Q4) A
Q5) A

Practice 3

You will hear a news item about a new educational initiative for underprivileged children.

Speaker: In an effort to bridge the educational gap and provide opportunities for underprivileged children, a nonprofit organization called EduConnect has launched a new initiative. The initiative, called "Education for All," aims to ensure access to quality education for children in low-income communities.

Through partnerships with local schools and community centers, EduConnect is setting up learning centers equipped with resources such as books, computers, and educational materials. These centers will serve as safe and supportive environments for children to study, receive tutoring, and engage in various educational activities.

The organization believes that education is a fundamental right and should not be limited by socioeconomic status. By providing equal access to educational resources and support, they aim to empower these children and give them the tools they need to succeed academically and beyond.

In addition to the physical learning centers, EduConnect is also implementing mentorship programs where volunteers from various professions will guide and inspire the children. The organization believes that positive role models and mentorship can have a significant impact on a child's educational journey and future prospects.

The "Education for All" initiative has received widespread support from the local community and businesses, with many offering donations, scholarships, and other forms of support to help ensure its success. The organization plans to expand its reach to more underserved areas and make a lasting difference in the lives of as many children as possible.

Q1) The news item is about...
A) a new initiative to provide education for underprivileged children.
B) the benefits of mentorship programs in education.
C) the importance of equal access to educational resources.
D) the success of a nonprofit organization.

Q2) What is the purpose of the learning centers set up by EduConnect?
A) To provide a safe environment for children to study.
B) To offer recreational activities for underprivileged children.
C) To provide job opportunities for local community members.
D) To establish partnerships with local businesses.

Q3) According to the news item, why is mentorship important in education?
A) It helps children receive tutoring and academic support.
B) It provides children with access to computers and books.
C) It empowers children and enhances their future prospects.
D) It encourages children to engage in educational activities.

Q4) How has the "Education for All" initiative been supported by the community?
A) Through offering scholarships to underprivileged children.
B) Through donating educational resources and materials.
C) Through organizing fundraising events.
D) Through providing volunteer mentors.

Q5) What are the future plans of EduConnect?
A) To establish more learning centers in underserved areas.
B) To focus on recreational activities for underprivileged children.
C) To provide job opportunities for volunteers.
D) To partner with international organizations for funding.

Answer key:

Q1) A
Q2) A

Q3) C
Q4) B
Q5) A

Part 5: Listening to a Discussion (8 Questions)

Part 5 of the Listening Test entails watching a video presentation where **3 individuals** engage in a conversation regarding a problem. However, there is a lack of consensus among them when it comes to finding a solution.

The speakers in the video could potentially be colleagues in a workplace setting or individuals collaborating as volunteers within a community.

This section aims to evaluate your listening skills in a more complex and interactive context. Here are the details and advanced tips to achieve a high score in this section:

Duration and Time Limit:
You are going to watch a **2-minute video** and next you are going to answer **8 questions**. The exact duration may vary slightly, but it is important to manage your time effectively to complete all the questions within the given timeframe.

Number of Questions:
Part 5 of the listening section consists of **8 questions**. Each question is based on a specific aspect or detail of the discussion. The questions may require you to identify the speakers' opinions, attitudes, main ideas, supporting details, or implications of the conversation. It is essential to listen carefully and grasp the key information to answer the questions accurately.

11 Tips and Strategies for Achieving a High Score

1. Pre-listening Preparation: Before the discussion begins, take a few moments to read through the questions and anticipate what you will be listening for. Familiarize yourself with the question types and the specific information you need to extract from the discussion.

2. Analyze the Context: Pay attention to the context and topic of the discussion. Understand the purpose and the main idea behind the conversation. This will help you grasp the overall meaning and enable you to answer questions related to the central theme effectively.

3. Identify Speaker Roles: During the discussion, try to identify the roles and relationships between the speakers. This can provide valuable context and assist in understanding the dynamics of the conversation. It may also help you determine the credibility or perspective of each speaker.

4. Listen for Implicit Information: In addition to explicit details, focus on capturing implicit information, such as tone, attitude, and implied meanings. Pay attention to the speakers' intonation, emphasis, and any non-verbal cues that can give you insights into their opinions or feelings.

5. Take Efficient Notes: While listening, take concise and organized notes to capture key information. Note down keywords, numbers, names, or any crucial details that might help you answer the questions accurately. Develop your shorthand or abbreviations to maximize efficiency.

6. Predict Answers: Before the answer choices are provided, try to predict the answer based on your understanding of the discussion. This can help you stay actively engaged and enhance your ability to recognize the correct response when it appears among the options.

7. Be Mindful of Similar Options: Pay close attention to the nuances and differences among the answer choices. Sometimes, there may be options that seem similar, but there will be subtle distinctions. Scrutinize the options to identify the one that aligns most accurately with the information presented in the discussion.

8. Use Process of Elimination: If you are unsure of the correct answer, use the process of elimination to eliminate obviously incorrect options. Narrowing down the choices can increase your chances of selecting the correct response, even if you are not entirely certain.

9. Practice Active Listening Skills: Develop your active listening skills by focusing on understanding the main ideas, supporting details, and inferences. Train your ears to pick up specific information while maintaining an awareness of the overall context.

10. Manage Time Effectively: Since there is no specific time limit per question, be mindful of your time management. Avoid spending excessive time on a single question that may cause you to rush through or omit later questions. Allocate your time based on the number of questions and maintain a steady pace throughout.

11. Review and Check Answers: If time permits, review your answers before moving on to the next section. Double-check your responses for accuracy, paying attention to any errors or inconsistencies. Be cautious of any careless mistakes or to misinterpretations.

By implementing these advanced tips and strategies, you can enhance your performance in the Listening to a Discussion section of the CELPIP test. Consistent practice, active listening skills, and effective time management will contribute to achieving a high score.

Remember to stay focused, extract key information, and analyze the context and speaker perspectives to select the most appropriate answers.

Practice 1

You will watch a discussion between three people at a cafe. They are talking about sustainable living.

Moderator: Welcome, everyone, to our panel discussion on sustainable living. Today, we have three experts who will share their insights and experiences. Let's start with Sarah. How do you define sustainable living?

Sarah: Thank you, moderator. Sustainable living, in my view, is about making choices that minimize our negative impact on the environment and promote long-term ecological balance. It involves conscious decisions regarding energy consumption, waste management, and the use of natural resources.

Moderator: That's a great definition, Sarah. Now, John, can you give us some examples of sustainable practices that individuals can adopt in their daily lives?

John: Absolutely, moderator. There are numerous ways individuals can contribute to sustainable living. Some examples include reducing energy consumption by using energy-efficient appliances, opting for renewable energy sources like solar power, practicing water conservation through methods like rainwater harvesting, and embracing eco-friendly transportation options like cycling or public transit.

Moderator: Thank you, John. Those are practical suggestions. Now, let's turn to Emma. How can sustainable living extend beyond individual choices to influence larger systems?

Emma: Excellent question, moderator. Sustainable living is not just about personal choices; it's also about advocating for systemic changes. By supporting sustainable businesses, engaging in local and national environmental initiatives, and demanding policy changes that prioritize sustainability, individuals can contribute to a broader shift towards a sustainable society. It's important to remember that collective action is crucial for lasting change.

Moderator: Well said, Emma. Now, let's discuss the challenges of sustainable living. John, what obstacles do people often face when trying to adopt sustainable practices?

John: One common challenge is the misconception that sustainable living is expensive or inconvenient. While it's true that some sustainable products may have higher upfront costs, they often lead to long-term savings. Additionally, lack of awareness and access to sustainable alternatives can hinder adoption. Education and government support are essential in overcoming these challenges and making sustainable living accessible to all.

Moderator: Thank you for addressing those obstacles, John. Now, Sarah, what benefits can individuals and communities experience by embracing sustainable living?

Sarah: Sustainable living brings numerous benefits. Personally, it helps individuals lead healthier lives, saves money in the long run, and fosters a sense of connection with the natural world. On a larger scale, sustainable living reduces pollution, preserves biodiversity, and mitigates climate change. It also promotes social equity and improves the overall well-being of communities.

Moderator: Thank you, Sarah. We have covered some valuable insights today. As we conclude, I encourage our audience to explore sustainable living practices and contribute to a more sustainable future. Remember, every small step counts.

That concludes our panel discussion on sustainable living. Thank you to our experts for sharing their knowledge and to our audience for joining us today.

Q1) How is sustainable living defined?
A) Maximizing energy consumption
B) Prioritizing economic growth
C) Minimizing negative impact on the environment

D) Promoting short-term ecological balance

Q2) Which of the following is an example of a sustainable practice?
A) Leaving lights on when not in use
B) Using disposable plastic water bottles
C) Opting for renewable energy sources
D) Driving a gas-guzzling SUV

Q3) How can individuals contribute to sustainable living beyond their personal choices?
A) Supporting sustainable businesses
B) Ignoring local and national environmental initiatives
C) Demanding policy changes that prioritize pollution
D) Encouraging wasteful consumption habits

Q4) What is one challenge people often face when adopting sustainable practices?
A) High upfront costs with no long-term savings
B) Lack of awareness and access to sustainable alternatives
C) The belief that sustainability is irrelevant
D) Government discouragement of sustainable living

Q5) What are some benefits of embracing sustainable living?
A) Increased pollution and biodiversity loss
B) Higher personal expenses and economic inequality
C) Improved health and cost savings
D) Social disconnection and community division

Q6) What can individuals do to contribute to a broader shift towards a sustainable society?
A) Ignore environmental initiatives and policies
B) Demand higher energy consumption
C) Advocate for systemic changes and support sustainable businesses
D) Consume non-renewable resources without restraint

Q7) How does sustainable living impact the environment?

A) It leads to increased pollution and resource depletion
B) It has no effect on biodiversity or climate change
C) It helps reduce pollution, preserve biodiversity, and mitigate climate change
D) It encourages wasteful consumption and disregard for natural resources

Q8) What is the importance of collective action in achieving sustainable living?
A) Collective action is unnecessary and ineffective
B) Individual choices alone are sufficient for sustainable living
C) Collective action is crucial for lasting change and a sustainable society
D) Sustainable living can only be achieved through government intervention

Answer key:

Q1) C
Q2) C
Q3) A
Q4) B
Q5) C
Q6) C
Q7) C
Q8) C

Practice 2

You will watch a discussion between three people at a cafe. They are talking about remote work and its benefits:

Moderator: Welcome, everyone, to our discussion on remote work. Today, we have three experts who will share their insights and experiences. Let's start with Mark. How would you define remote work?

Mark: Thank you, moderator. Remote work refers to the practice of working outside of a traditional office environment, often from home or any location with internet access. It allows individuals to perform their job responsibilities without being physically present in a centralized workspace.

Moderator: That's a great definition, Mark. Now, Sarah, could you highlight some of the benefits of remote work for individuals and companies?

Sarah: Absolutely, moderator. Remote work offers numerous advantages. For individuals, it provides flexibility in managing their work-life balance, eliminates commuting time and associated stress, and allows them to create a personalized and comfortable work environment. From a company's perspective, remote work increases employee satisfaction and productivity, reduces overhead costs, and enables access to a wider pool of talent regardless of geographical limitations.

Moderator: Thank you, Sarah. Those are compelling benefits. Now, let's turn to John. What challenges do remote workers often face, and how can they be addressed?

John: Excellent question, moderator. Remote workers may encounter challenges such as feelings of isolation, blurred work-life boundaries, and the need for effective communication and collaboration. To address these challenges, companies can prioritize regular team check-ins and foster a strong virtual community. It's essential for individuals to establish clear boundaries, create a designated workspace, and make an effort to connect with colleagues through virtual platforms. Emphasizing communication and using the right tools can help overcome these challenges effectively.

Moderator: Thank you, John. Now, let's discuss the impact of remote work on company culture. Mark, how does remote work influence the overall company culture?

Mark: Remote work certainly has an impact on company culture, moderator. It challenges traditional norms by emphasizing flexibility, trust, and results-driven approaches. Remote work promotes a culture of autonomy, accountability, and self-discipline. It requires companies to redefine how they foster employee engagement, build strong relationships, and maintain a sense of belonging and shared purpose. Embracing digital communication tools and virtual team-building activities can help nurture a positive and inclusive company culture in a remote work environment.

Moderator: Well said, Mark. Now, let's address the future of remote work. Sarah, do you believe that remote work will continue to grow in popularity, and what trends do you foresee?

Sarah: Absolutely, moderator. Remote work has gained significant momentum, and I believe it will continue to grow in popularity. The COVID-19 pandemic has accelerated the adoption of remote work, and many companies have realized the benefits it brings. Going forward, we may see a hybrid work model emerge, combining remote and in-office work. The focus will be on providing employees with flexibility and choice while leveraging technology to facilitate seamless collaboration and communication.

Moderator: Thank you, Sarah. We have explored some valuable insights today. As we conclude, I encourage our audience to embrace the opportunities and overcome the challenges of remote work. Remember, it's a dynamic and evolving landscape that can bring numerous benefits when managed effectively.

That concludes our discussion on remote work. Thank you to our experts for sharing their knowledge and to our audience for joining us today.

Q1) How is remote work defined?
A) Working in a traditional office environment
B) Working from any location without internet access
C) Working from home or outside a centralized workspace
D) Working without any job responsibilities

Q2) What are some benefits of remote work for individuals?
A) Increased commuting time and stress
B) Limited work-life balance
C) Access to a wider pool of talent
D) Reduced employee satisfaction

Q3) How does remote work benefit companies?
A) Decreased employee productivity
B) Higher overhead costs
C) Limited talent pool
D) Increased employee satisfaction and productivity

Q4) What challenges do remote workers often face?
A) Strong work-life boundaries
B) Limited communication and collaboration
C) Physical presence in a centralized workspace
D) Less sense of isolation

Q5) How can remote workers address the challenge of isolation?
A) Establishing clear boundaries
B) Creating a designated workspace
C) Regular team check-ins and virtual community
D) Avoiding communication and virtual platforms

Q6) How does remote work influence company culture?
A) Emphasizes flexibility, trust, and results-driven approaches

B) Strengthens traditional norms and practices
C) Negatively impacts employee engagement
D) Reduces the need for effective communication

Q7) Do experts believe remote work will continue to grow in popularity?
A) No, it will decline in popularity
B) Yes, it will continue to grow in popularity
C) It will remain stagnant with no changes
D) The popularity of remote work is irrelevant

Q8) What trend is expected in the future of remote work?
A) Elimination of remote work options
B) Hybrid work model combining remote and in-office work
C) No changes in work models
D) Decreased reliance on technology for communication

Answer key:

Q1) C
Q2) C
Q3) D
Q4) B
Q5) C
Q6) A
Q7) B
Q8) B

Practice 3

You will watch a discussion between three people at a cafe. They are talking about healthy eating and nutrition:

Moderator: Welcome, everyone, to our discussion on healthy eating and nutrition. Today, we have three experts who will share their insights and tips. Let's start with Lisa. How would you define healthy eating?

Lisa: Thank you, moderator. Healthy eating is about consuming a well-balanced diet that provides essential nutrients, vitamins, and minerals for optimal health. It involves incorporating a variety of fruits, vegetables, whole grains, lean proteins, and healthy fats into our meals while limiting processed foods, added sugars, and unhealthy fats.

Moderator: That's a great definition, Lisa. Now, let's turn to John. What are some key benefits of healthy eating for our overall well-being?

John: Absolutely, moderator. Healthy eating offers numerous benefits. It supports weight management, reduces the risk of chronic diseases such as heart disease and diabetes, enhances our immune system, improves energy levels, and promotes mental clarity. It also contributes to healthy aging and a better quality of life.

Moderator: Thank you, John. Those are important benefits. Now, let's discuss common challenges people face when trying to maintain a healthy diet. Sarah, what are some obstacles and how can they be overcome?

Sarah: Excellent question, moderator. People often face challenges such as busy schedules, limited access to fresh and nutritious foods, and cravings for unhealthy options. To overcome these obstacles, it's important to plan and prioritize meals in advance, incorporate meal prepping and batch cooking, and choose healthier alternatives when eating out. Additionally, building a support system, seeking guidance from nutrition professionals, and practicing mindful eating can help overcome challenges and establish sustainable healthy eating habits.

Moderator: Thank you, Sarah. Now, let's talk about the role of portion control in healthy eating. Lisa, how important is portion control, and what strategies can individuals use?

Lisa: Portion control plays a crucial role in maintaining a healthy diet, moderator. It helps ensure that we consume appropriate amounts of food and manage calorie intake. Some strategies individuals can use include measuring and weighing food portions, using smaller plates and bowls to visually control portions, and practicing mindful eating by paying attention to hunger and fullness cues. It's also helpful to educate ourselves about appropriate portion sizes for different food groups.

Moderator: Thank you, Lisa. Now, let's address the topic of food labels. John, how can individuals make informed choices by reading and understanding food labels?

John: Reading and understanding food labels is essential for making informed choices, moderator. Individuals should look for key information such as serving size, calorie content, nutrient breakdown, and ingredients list. It's important to pay attention to added sugars, unhealthy fats, and artificial additives. Comparing labels and opting for products with lower sodium, sugar, and saturated fat content can contribute to a healthier diet.

Moderator: Thank you, John. As we conclude, I encourage our audience to prioritize healthy eating by incorporating nutritious foods into their daily meals. Remember, small changes can lead to significant improvements in our overall well-being.

That concludes our discussion on healthy eating and nutrition. Thank you to our experts for sharing their knowledge and to our audience for joining us today.

Q1) How would you define healthy eating?
A) Consuming a diet high in processed foods and added sugars
B) Following a strict calorie-restricted diet
C) Incorporating a variety of nutritious foods into meals
D) Focusing solely on weight loss

Q2) What are some key benefits of healthy eating?
A) Increased risk of chronic diseases
B) Reduced energy levels and mental clarity
C) Improved weight management and immune system
D) Promotion of unhealthy aging

Q3) What challenges do people face when trying to maintain a healthy diet?
A) Limited access to fresh and nutritious foods
B) Excessive portion control and calorie counting
C) Embracing cravings for unhealthy options
D) Relying on nutrition professionals for guidance

Q4) How can individuals overcome challenges to maintain a healthy diet?
A) Ignoring meal planning and preparation
B) Prioritizing convenience over nutrition
C) Seeking support and practicing mindful eating
D) Avoiding healthy alternatives when eating out

Q5) How important is portion control in healthy eating?
A) Not important, as long as the food is nutritious
B) It plays a crucial role in maintaining a healthy diet
C) Portion control only affects weight loss goals
D) Portion control has no impact on overall well-being

Q6) What strategies can individuals use for portion control?
A) Avoiding meal prepping and batch cooking
B) Using larger plates to visually control portions
C) Measuring and weighing food portions
D) Ignoring hunger and fullness cues

Q7) How can individuals make informed choices by reading food labels?
A) Disregarding serving size and calorie content
B) Paying attention to added sugars and unhealthy fats
C) Not comparing labels and choosing products at random
D) Focusing on artificial additives and preservatives

Q8) What should individuals consider when reading food labels?
A) Nutrient breakdown and ingredients list
B) Ignoring sodium, sugar, and saturated fat content
C) Opting for products with high levels of additives
D) Not paying attention to serving size information

Answer key:

Q1) C
Q2) C
Q3) A
Q4) C
Q5) B
Q6) C
Q7) B
Q8) A

Part 6: Listening to Viewpoints (6 Questions)

In Part 6 of the CELPIP Listening section, which is called "Listening to Viewpoints," you will listen to a recording of a conversation between two people expressing their opinions or viewpoints on a particular topic.

This section aims to assess your ability to understand and interpret different perspectives and opinions.

Timing:
Part 6 typically takes around 6-7 minutes to complete, including the time for listening to the recording and answering the questions. You will hear a report once which is about 3 minutes long. Then 6 questions will appear.

Number of Questions:
There are a total of 6 questions in Part 6 of the CELPIP Listening section. Each question corresponds to a specific viewpoint or opinion expressed in the conversation.

Answering Time:
After listening to the conversation, you will have a short period of time to answer each question. The exact time given for each question may vary, but it is usually around 10-20 seconds per question. It's important to manage your time effectively to ensure you answer all the questions within the given time frame.

7 Tips and Strategies for a High Score

1. Focus on the main ideas: Pay close attention to the main ideas and arguments presented in the conversation. Understanding the overall message will help you answer the questions accurately.

2. Take effective notes: Use abbreviations, symbols, or keywords to jot down important points while listening. This will help you recall and organize information when answering the questions.

3. Understand different viewpoints: The conversation may present contrasting opinions or viewpoints. Listen carefully to identify the speaker's stance and how they support their viewpoint. This will assist you in selecting the correct answers.

4. Watch for signal words: Pay attention to signal words or phrases that indicate contrasting viewpoints, such as "however," "on the other hand," or "in contrast." These words can help you identify the shift in perspectives and choose the appropriate response.

5. Use the process of elimination: If you are unsure about an answer, try eliminating options that are clearly incorrect. Narrowing down the choices can increase your chances of selecting the correct response.

6. Practice active listening: Train your listening skills by engaging in regular listening exercises or activities. This can involve listening to podcasts, TED Talks, or other recordings where multiple viewpoints are presented.

7. Familiarize yourself with different topics: Read and listen to various materials on different topics to expose yourself to a range of perspectives. This will enhance your ability to understand and interpret viewpoints effectively during the test.

Remember to familiarize yourself with the CELPIP Listening format and practice using sample tests to get accustomed to the time constraints and question types. Building your listening skills and applying effective strategies will contribute to achieving a high score in Part 6 of the CELPIP Listening section.

Practice 1

You will hear a report about the use of genetically modified organisms (GMOs) in agriculture:

Genetically modified organisms, or GMOs, have been a subject of debate and controversy in the agricultural industry for many years. GMOs are organisms whose genetic material has been altered in a way that does not occur naturally through traditional breeding methods. This modification is typically done to introduce specific traits or characteristics into crops or livestock.

Proponents of GMOs argue that these genetically engineered organisms offer numerous benefits to farmers and consumers alike. They claim that GMOs can enhance crop yields, increase resistance to pests and diseases, and improve the nutritional content of food. Additionally, they argue that GMOs have the potential to address global food security challenges by producing crops that can thrive in harsh environmental conditions.

However, critics express concerns about the potential risks and negative consequences associated with the use of GMOs. They argue that the long-term effects of consuming genetically modified foods on human health and the environment are not yet fully understood. Some opponents of GMOs also raise ethical concerns about the ownership and control of genetically modified seeds by large corporations, which they believe can limit farmers' choices and perpetuate an unsustainable agricultural system.

To delve deeper into this issue, let's hear different viewpoints on the topic:

Interviewee 1: Sarah Thompson, a farmer who has been growing genetically modified crops for several years, emphasizes the benefits of GMOs. According to her, genetically engineered crops have helped her increase her farm's productivity, reduce the need for chemical pesticides, and improve the quality of her produce. She believes that GMOs have the potential to revolutionize agriculture and contribute to a more sustainable and efficient food production system.

Interviewee 2: Dr. Mark Roberts, a renowned environmental scientist, expresses concerns about the risks associated with GMOs. He points out that the use of genetically modified crops can lead to unintended consequences, such as the development of superweeds or the loss of biodiversity. Dr. Roberts argues that more research and long-term studies are needed to fully understand the environmental impacts and potential health risks of GMOs before they are widely adopted.

Interviewee 3: Julia Ramirez, a consumer and advocate for organic farming, questions the transparency and labeling practices related to GMOs. She believes that consumers have the right to know whether the food they purchase contains genetically modified ingredients. Julia argues that proper labeling allows individuals to make informed choices about the products they consume and supports the principle of consumer sovereignty.

As the debate on GMOs continues, it is crucial to consider the scientific evidence, ethical implications, and societal impacts associated with their use.

Apologies for the oversight. Here are the revised multiple-choice questions for the script:

Q1) GMOs refer to organisms that have been genetically modified in a way that does not occur naturally through traditional breeding methods. Is this statement:
A) True
B) False

Q2) Proponents of GMOs claim that they can help address which of the following challenges?
A) Water scarcity
B) Global food security
C) Climate change

D) Biodiversity conservation

Q3) Critics of GMOs raise concerns about their potential long-term effects on:
A) Human health and the environment
B) Crop yields and productivity
C) Genetic diversity in livestock
D) Market competitiveness of organic farming

Q4) Sarah Thompson, a farmer, believes that GMOs have improved the quality of her produce and reduced the need for:
A) Synthetic fertilizers
B) Chemical pesticides
C) Irrigation water
D) Genetic modification

Q5) Dr. Mark Roberts emphasizes the need for more research to fully understand the:
A) Economic impacts of GMOs
B) Consumer demand for GMO-labeled products
C) Environmental impacts and potential health risks of GMOs
D) Relationship between GMOs and agricultural subsidies

Q6) Julia Ramirez advocates for proper labeling of genetically modified products to enable consumers to make informed choices regarding:
A) Nutritional content
B) Organic certifications
C) Country of origin
D) Genetic modification status

Answer key:

Q1) A
Q2) B
Q3) A
Q4) B
Q5) C

Q6) D

Practice 2

You will hear a report about the impact of social media on society:

Social media platforms have become an integral part of our daily lives, with billions of people actively using platforms like Facebook, Instagram, Twitter, and Snapchat. While social media has undeniably transformed the way we communicate and access information, it has also sparked numerous debates regarding its impact on society.

Supporters of social media argue that it has brought people closer together, allowing us to connect with friends, family, and acquaintances regardless of geographical distance. They highlight how social media has facilitated the sharing of ideas, photos, and experiences, fostering a sense of community and promoting social activism. Furthermore, they claim that social media has given a voice to marginalized individuals and provided a platform for grassroots movements and social change.

However, critics raise concerns about the negative effects of social media on mental health, privacy, and social interactions. They argue that excessive use of social media can lead to feelings of loneliness, anxiety, and depression. Moreover, they point out that social media platforms often collect vast amounts of personal data, raising privacy and security concerns. Critics also highlight the detrimental impact of cyberbullying and the spread of misinformation through social media, which can have severe consequences for individuals and society at large.

To gain further insight into this topic, let's listen to different viewpoints on the impact of social media:

Interviewee 1: John Anderson, a social media enthusiast and influencer, believes that social media has revolutionized the way we communicate and interact. He emphasizes the positive aspects, such as the ability to connect with diverse communities, share knowledge, and promote social causes. John argues that social media empowers individuals and amplifies their voices, leading to positive societal change.

Interviewee 2: Dr. Emily Thompson, a psychologist specializing in mental health, expresses concerns about the negative effects of social media on well-being. She highlights the addictive nature of social media and its potential to amplify feelings of inadequacy and social comparison. Dr. Thompson emphasizes the importance of setting healthy boundaries and using social media mindfully to protect mental health.

Interviewee 3: Sarah Johnson, a privacy advocate and cybersecurity expert, raises concerns about the privacy implications of social media. She argues that social media platforms have access to vast amounts of personal data, which can be exploited for targeted advertising and surveillance purposes. Sarah stresses the need for stronger privacy regulations and user control over personal data.

As the debate on the impact of social media continues, it is crucial to evaluate its benefits and drawbacks.

Q1) Social media platforms have transformed the way we communicate and access information. Is this statement:
A) True
B) False
C) Partially true
D) Uncertain

Q2) Supporters of social media argue that it fosters a sense of community and promotes:
A) Loneliness
B) Social activism
C) Information overload
D) Face-to-face interactions

Q3) Critics raise concerns about the negative effects of social media on:

A) Mental health and privacy
B) Physical fitness and productivity
C) Global politics and economy
D) Traditional media and journalism

Q4) John Anderson believes that social media empowers individuals and amplifies their voices, leading to:
A) Negative societal change
B) Decreased online engagement
C) Social isolation
D) Positive societal change

Q5) Dr. Emily Thompson emphasizes the importance of using social media:
A) Excessively for social comparison
B) Mindfully and with healthy boundaries
C) To seek validation and self-worth
D) Without considering mental health implications

Q6) Sarah Johnson advocates for stronger privacy regulations and user control over personal data on social media platforms. Is this statement:
A) True
B) False
C) Partially true
D) Uncertain

Answer key:

Q1) A
Q2) B
Q3) A
Q4)D
Q5) B
Q6) A

Practice 3

You will hear a report about the impact of renewable energy on the environment:

Renewable energy sources, such as solar, wind, hydro, and geothermal power, have gained significant attention as alternatives to traditional fossil fuel-based energy. Proponents of renewable energy highlight its potential to mitigate climate change, reduce greenhouse gas emissions, and promote sustainable development. However, there are ongoing debates surrounding the efficacy and implications of renewable energy sources.

Supporters argue that renewable energy is environmentally friendly and offers a solution to the challenges posed by fossil fuels. They emphasize that harnessing renewable energy can significantly reduce carbon emissions, decrease air and water pollution, and minimize the ecological footprint of energy production. Additionally, they claim that investing in renewable energy technologies can stimulate economic growth, create job opportunities, and enhance energy security.

However, critics raise concerns about the limitations and drawbacks of renewable energy sources. They argue that renewable technologies can be expensive to implement and maintain, requiring substantial investments. Critics also highlight issues related to intermittency, as renewable energy production relies on weather conditions and geographical factors. Furthermore, some argue that the large-scale deployment of renewable energy infrastructure can have adverse ecological and visual impacts on landscapes and habitats.

To gain further insight into this topic, let's listen to different viewpoints on the impact of renewable energy:

Interviewee 1: John Adams, an environmental activist, strongly supports the adoption of renewable energy. He believes that renewable sources can lead to a cleaner, healthier environment by reducing carbon emissions and dependence on fossil fuels. John emphasizes the importance of transitioning to renewable energy to combat climate change and promote sustainable development.

Interviewee 2: Dr. Emily Carter, a renewable energy researcher, acknowledges the benefits of renewable energy but also recognizes its limitations. She highlights the need for further research and technological advancements to address intermittency issues and improve energy storage technologies. Dr. Carter emphasizes the importance of a balanced energy mix and the integration of renewable energy into existing power systems.

Interviewee 3: Sarah Johnson, an economist, raises concerns about the economic feasibility of renewable energy. She argues that while renewable sources have long-term benefits, the initial investment costs can be substantial. Sarah advocates for comprehensive cost-benefit analyses and strategic planning to ensure the economic viability and sustainability of renewable energy projects.

Q1) Renewable energy sources aim to:
A) Increase carbon emissions
B) Promote sustainable development
C) Depend on fossil fuels
D) Create energy security challenges

Q2) Critics of renewable energy express concerns about its:
A) Expensive implementation and maintenance
B) Positive impact on job opportunities
C) Ability to reduce air and water pollution
D) Reliance on weather conditions

Q3) John Adams supports renewable energy as a means to combat:
A) Economic growth
B) Climate change
C) Energy security

D) Fossil fuel dependence

Q4) Dr. Emily Carter emphasizes the importance of addressing the issue of:
A) Environmental pollution
B) Renewable energy integration
C) Economic feasibility
D) Technological advancements

Q5) Sarah Johnson advocates for comprehensive cost-benefit analyses to ensure the:
A) Economic viability of renewable energy
B) Ecological impact of renewable technologies
C) Promotion of job opportunities
D) Reduction of carbon emissions

Q6) The report mentions that renewable energy technologies can have adverse impacts on:
A) Economic growth
B) Climate change mitigation
C) Ecological landscapes
D) Fossil fuel dependence"

Answer key:

Q1) B
Q2) A
Q3) B
Q4) D
Q5) A
Q6) C

Final Words

As you reach the end of this CELPIP Listening book, I want to extend my heartfelt congratulations to all of you on your journey to success in the CELPIP test. Your dedication and commitment to improving your language skills are commendable.

Remember, practice is the key to achieving your desired results. Make it a habit to set aside 30 minutes to 1 hour every day for focused practice on the listening section. Engage with various listening materials, such as recordings, podcasts, and conversations, to enhance your listening comprehension skills.

Immerse yourself in the language, paying attention to pronunciation, intonation, and vocabulary usage. Take advantage of practice tests and exercises included in this book, as they provide valuable opportunities to refine your listening abilities.

Always remember that progress takes time, effort, and consistency. Be patient with yourself and celebrate the small victories along the way. Each day of practice brings you closer to your goals.

I wish you all the best in your CELPIP test. May your hard work and dedication yield outstanding results. Trust in your abilities, stay focused, and approach the test with confidence. You have the skills and determination to excel.

Believe in yourself, practice diligently, and success will undoubtedly be within your reach.

Best regards,

Ali Rastegari

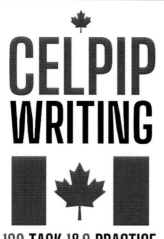

CELPIP WRITING
100 TASK 1&2 PRACTICE TOPICS WITH ANSWERS
TARGET CLB 10+

CELPIP SPEAKING
TOP TIPS & TEMPLATES TO PASS SPEAKING TASKS
TARGET CLB 10+

CELPIP READING
TOP TIPS & STRATEGIES WITH PRACTICE TESTS
TARGET CLB 10+

CELPIP VOCABULARY
TOP 500 WORDS YOU MUST KNOW TO PASS CELPIP TEST
TARGET CLB 10+

Manufactured by Amazon.ca
Acheson, AB